Worshipping at Lenin's Mausoleum

Judith A. Rypma

FUTURECYCLE PRESS
www.futurecycle.org

Copyright © 2016 Judith A. Rypma
All Rights Reserved

Published by FutureCycle Press
Lexington, Kentucky, USA

ISBN 978-1-942371-21-2

Contents

The Russians Are Coming: 1962 5
Soviet-Style Touring, 1982 7
Worshipping at Lenin's Mausoleum 10
Touring the Ukraine, 1988 12
Place of Wood 13
A Russian Tale, 1990 15
The Early 1990s, Russian Federation 17
Happy Endings 19
2004: The Information Age Arrives in Russia 20
To Elena, Thirty Years Later 21
The Amber Room: Pushkin, Russia 22
In Stalin's Bunker, Samara 28
Baba Yaga 30
Baba Yaga and Me 32
Maiden's Island 35
Volga River 37
Reflections While Viewing Catherine the Great's Jewels 39
Living at The Five Corners, St. Petersburg, 2016 41

The Russians Are Coming: 1962

Teachers never told us
which was which
arrival of the dreaded Commies
or
the ten-minute air raid drill

so when sirens pierced air
we needed to clap hands to ears
but no time to wait out
the awful noise. No time
to kneel for yet another prayer
the Soviet Union would not
burn us all with nuclear weapons
or at least take over our country
before we could grow up, go to high school.

My parents couldn't afford a bomb shelter
but someone decided
I lived close enough to get home
even if blasted to kingdom come
before reaching our basement finishing line.

It was as if someone fired a starting pistol

though this was no foot race
but a terrified take off
from the elementary classroom
at breakneck speed
bobby socks bunching around ankles
nearly tripping over scuffed saddle shoes.

so legs separating like giant scissors

I ran a marathon

dashed past the sliding board
did a relay around the teeter totter
hurdled railroad tracks
sprinted back alleys
jumped ditches
rounded the second suburban block

would not think to wonder
until decades and decades later
why my entire class
didn't form our own track team.

Soviet-Style Touring, 1982

It is a Last Frontier
for tourists. Forbidden Zone
of restrictions
discomforts
dangers

like daring to leave the hotel
at three in the morning
in a fruitless search for all-night coffee

or getting caught smuggling in
an issue of *Cosmopolitan*
raising a Pentax to get a shot
of a high level Kremlin delegation
until a cacophony of shouts, whistles
convinces my husband to forego
capturing Brezhnev on film.

not jumping out of our skin
when an overzealous soldier blows a whistle
because one of our group strayed
from precise chalk lines
controlling movement on Red Square's pavement

yet the real risks

were maneuvering a sea of umbrellas
without losing an eye

or getting lost forever
following the deceptive tourist map labeled Moscow

so many deliberate errors it might as well
be a grid of Dublin

or attempting to ignore offers
to purchase our jeans, change rubles for dollars

tackling the Cyrillic alphabet
especially in the labyrinthic subway

seeking hidden microphones, cameras
that never revealed themselves

not slamming down the phone
after middle of night bed checks
in a sterile hotel with hall monitors

slipping a forbidden tip (always Marlboros or Doublemint)
to a friendly yet nervous waiter

no this
no that
allowed

If it's two, this must be the Sparrow Hills

until we are at last compelled
to go AWOL
probably reported to the KGB
by the Intourist guide trained for such things
the one who claims not to know what happened to the last tsar
replies vaguely he is buried *Somewhere up North*

yet so much to see
so many misconceptions

and that first time here

no way to predict
someday
someone here would know the word purge
the hotel band will have heard of
Lara's Theme, Dr. Zhivago, Pasternak
there would be no more Swiss Cheese history

we wouldn't be constrained
by the regiment.

No way to foresee
all the Stalin posters, labor banners, Brezhnev portraits
would be ripped down
Lenin statues peopling every square
soon toppling into the past's thick dust

so instead accepted
endless queues
for something no one at the back
could identify

the woman ahead of me in line turning
to reveal missing teeth
a Jack-O-lantern face
still bright and rotund
as the gilded cupolas
clustered in the distance—

giant droplets of gold
on cathedrals splashed
with centuries of sunlight.

Worshipping at Lenin's Mausoleum

Shuffling along praying
for this endless serpentine line
to draw closer

to the black and blood granite altar
holiest consecrated shrine

while uniformed apostles
murmur a litany:
hats off, no talking

blow a choir of whistles
to keep pilgrims
from straying.

Downstairs more clergy
urge us to move along—
no time to kneel
genuflect, cross oneself
solve the mystery
of afterlife

just a brief glance
at the principal relic—
best funeral suit and tie
illuminated red halo
feet aimed
at Red Square.

No pause permitted
at the icon
though guards eye my purse

as if at any moment
I might whip out a rosary

worse yet a weapon
to fire at God's body
prevent him
from a Resurrection.

Touring the Ukraine, 1988

Passing refineries and coal mines
our Intourist guide explains the evils
imposed by tsars, nobles, states, raiders
and we nod slightly, as if we don't know

about such things: vegetative guillotines,
great pushes forward, township officials
paid to approve Five-Year Plans
while from the front seat our host waves

toward a leftover sign: *Glory to Labor*
while we products of the Midwest's
mixed marriage of bread and steel
ooh and *ah* over storks ensconced

in straw rooftop mansions. The guide shrugs
as if they'll nest there forever. Does not want
to talk about bits of Chernobyl
filtering through the Dnieper's silt.

I consider asking the driver to pull over
unload us all in the middle of
bloody blessed nowhere
where together we could fill buckets

with sweet black cherries
sit beside the uneven road stroking
the storks' feathers. Cradling the last
sheaves of golden summer wheat.

Place of Wood

First day in Armenia
craving a taste of golden ears
steaming in a bucket
but nothing to offer
the corn cob seller
crouched beside the road
on a hairpin mountain turn

emptied pockets
of wrappers, pencil stubs, gum
finally found a trade: one box
of stick matches

left satisfied, gnawing
my prize. Not realizing
until days later
the value of wood:

Teakwood barrels of brandy
for easing pain of remembrance.
Kindling for outlasting an embargo.
Planks that split apart
when the earth opened.
Bark for death march dining.

One stick used
by a Roman soldier to lance
Christ's side.
One preserved, polished slice
of Noah's waterlogged Ark.

One twig
that produced a fruit tree
for two people who harvested it
paid
the ultimate price—
still a bargain
if they had heeded
the knowledge it yielded.

A Russian Tale, 1990

She could be a puppet
propped against the Kremlin wall:
tangled, unwashed pigtails
grimy, faded Raggedy Ann pinafore
dulled candy eyes
of someone's forgotten toy.

Above her ruby stars
glow less brightly
last year's tarnished Christmas tree toppers
still lording it over
clusters of golden domes
like balloons unwilling to burst

yet still maintaining the holy sheen
that once bedazzled peasants
begging a tsar for crumbs.

Years from now
the tent city will have vanished
quickly as the wizard floated away
without Dorothy

and her face
will hover in my memory
reminding me I am not
Glinda
could not have waved a sparkling wand
lifting either of us
to the world we want

an Oz that promises
to fulfill our hearts' desires.

"Twelve years old," it says
on the muddied cardboard scrap
dangling like a price tag from her neck
though she clutches it tightly
as any child would clasp
a wish list for parents
to replace the ones sent south
banished like so many before
from the elusive kingdom

leaving behind
a would-be princess
and leftover dreams
from an out-of-print storybook.

The Early 1990s, Russian Federation

Glasnost carefully painted
on *matrysohka* dolls
    though Gorbachev now nests inside
Yeltsin's chubby face and figure
        a teensy Lenin contained within

Lines less urgent
    vodka forbidden
            all else revealed

      or so it would seem

stores carrying *Gulag Archipelago*
beside unsold issues of *Pravda*

newly crowded cathedrals

teens hawking military uniforms
kiosks openly displaying
            porn   more on the Arbat
where street artists manage to embarrass me

hurrying past new graves
    Brezhnev   Andropov   Chernenko
joining
Stalin   Reed   the usual assortment
of cosmonauts
scientists
Party officials

lines to Lenin's squatting tomb
less urgent than those
at newly opened cooperative stores

entrepreneurs wearing imperial armbands
    selling photographs   of the last Romanov children
outside *Moscow News* offices

the new red, white, and blue flag
fluttering above the Senate's dome

Lady, good price for you

a young man insists
waving a KGB shirt

when I shake my head
produces a leftover one
emblazoned with *perestroika*

Nyet, spacibo

but someone else replaces him
offers cheap jars of salmon caviar
secured from a friend of a friend
who works at a tourist hotel

the past revised hourly   and I don't know where to look
    next

in this nation of daily shifting
        reshifting
the way bits, pieces
of colored glass and beads
    tumble
        in unexpected patterns
rearranging themselves
with each twist
of the kaleidoscope's wheel.

Happy Endings

It seems as if a hundred years passed
before they removed barbed wire
like thorns protecting
the Soviet border. Yet still
the Faithful, curious
file into Red Square
seeking admittance
to the rose and gray granite castle
guarding the prince
of communism. Inside
the mausoleum
Lenin is propped on a pillow
unaware
that when he pricked his finger
an entire nation
bled with him
fell under the same curse
that put everyone to sleep
for decades.
Not realizing
chances are good
no one will ever want
to awaken him
with or without
a kiss.

2004: The Information Age Arrives in Russia

His caretaker admitted this year
that Vladimir's Ilych Lenin's genitals
are still intact

which is more than anyone
should want to know
though better

than knowing nothing
the way it used to be.

To Elena, Thirty Years Later

That day she stood alone in the Uglich churchyard, framed by a field of dandelions passing as wildflowers. Displayed a handful of paintings, the only local resident to take *glasnost* and *perestroika* seriously. Apprentice wizard with watercolors. I proffered a handful of Russian words, a few rubles. Transaction concluded with smiles, a photo. Never dreamed we'd meet again. Nothing else to say—or buy, except from a store hawking watches that stopped working a month later. A few *babushkas* selling dahlias and gladioli lined the dock as we sailed. Did not look up. The painting of the Church on the Blood hung in my bedroom for decades.

This time the ship disengorges passengers at the beginning of the yellow brick road of tourism. Hundreds of vendors border the pier, culminating in an Emerald City of watch and jewelry shops. Time has marched ahead a hundred years. Elena stands between them all, older and wiser. I recognize her with the help of that photo taken when she, I, and Russia were much younger. We manage an entire conversation this time. Laugh at our younger selves. Promise to exchange emails. I discover tears in my eyes when I leave. Take comfort in recalling that in the sequels, Baum sent Dorothy back to Oz.

The Amber Room: Pushkin, Russia

> *"Some people have princesses & fairies. Others have the Amber Room."*
> —Professor Wolfgang Eichwede

I.

Too busy playing war games
Peter the Great ignored his giant gift
left his female successors
to patch the chamber together

so decades later Catherine the Great
ordered a half ton of amber
shipped from East Prussia. Hired a quartet
of carvers to replace fakes,
eight mosaics to fill pilaster holes
profusely enrich it with royal monograms,
garlands of seashells, fruits in shades
of banana, pear, lemon, cantaloupe
flowers in sunflower, daffodil, primrose, poppy,
marigold hues. Butterscotch ribbons
three-dimensional mythic carvings
masked cartouches, imperial crowns.

Two hundred fifty shades in all
until the Eighth Wonder of the World
emerged in all its baroque glory
upper tiers embellished with
candelabra crowded with golden cupids
walls hung with allegorical Roman scenes
from jasper, onyx, nephrite, lapis lazuli

framed in a sparkling kaleidoscope
of smoky quartz, citrine, topaz, ruby.

Gilded white doors, parquet floors
swirled with mother-of-pearl
parrots and eagles soaring on antique friezes
classical ceiling painting illuminated
by twinkling chandeliers, five hundred candles

sun pouring through wide windows
reflecting off mirrors—enough light
to blind Saul on his way to Damascus.

II.

Nazi art brigades swooped in
galloped through Catherine's Palace
unsaddled horses
in empty gilded rooms.

Knowing what they wanted
they needed only minutes
to rip it off

then rape and kidnap
the treasured walls hidden
beneath a thin paper disguise.

They shipped it all to Prussia
where it would disappear.
Launch a thousand searches
worthy of the ones
for the holy grail—impossible
to find, impossible to forget.

III.

The recreation required decades
by a team of over fifty
overwhelmed by six tons of amber

moving gradually, meticulously
guided by only a few grainy photos
blown up life size.
Ignorant of lost techniques
they experimented with every step
constructed a model to precise scale
made six volumes of drawings

so often must have despaired
of the ultimate challenge:
restoring the original's sumptuous mystique.

Bent over microscopes
they might as well have tried
to recreate the Fabergé eggs
or remake the universe
in a mere seven days.

Trial runs on postage-stamp size pieces
three months to test gem curvature
on a Florentine mosaic. Over a hundred
test cycles to discover beeswax produces
the best glue if adhered with hair dryers.

Years poring over archives
from a former lapidary factory
and medieval amber guilds

no interior designer
could have worked harder
or summoned so many artists, librarians,
art critics, archaeologists, stone cutters.

Two thousand miniature patterns
for one panel. Dyed color combos
matched and tried like paint samples
or wallpaper swatches.

The workshop resembled
an alchemist's laboratory
with flasks and pots of amber
various oils, herbs
boiling, steaming, bubbling

each piece carefully carved
to exact thickness and shape
before being polished
fitted into a precise slot
to reassemble Peter the Great's
massive royal puzzle
Catherine's and Russia's
beloved crown jewel.

IV.

Another decade passed
before I set foot inside

knowing then if angels exist
these must be their colors

bathing me in streams
of spiritual golden light.
No iconostasis so rich

shimmering sunshine shades
flowing from warm walls

to caress the body
baptize the soul

with this mixture
of butter, brandy, paprika,
lemon, honey, root beer
banana, tangerine, Riesling

until worshipping isn't enough.
I need a taste

to sip it in a chalice
lay it on my tongue.

Sinking to the parquet floor
I'm not the same
as before. Have reached
my own state of grace

now that, like Ezekiel,
I have seen heaven

yearn to be embalmed
in amber. My ashes mixed
within these walls

entombed here for eternity
one more tiny time capsule
of the past. One more
piece of the heavenly host.

In Stalin's Bunker, Samara

I.

Russian officials discovered
its location in the nineties
this place he planned to hunker down
to oversee Stalingrad's Last Stand

an underground fortress
built by six hundred workers
laboring twelve hours a day
sans machines. Scrabbling
in dirt with fingers, shovels.

Confined to the yard
of an innocuous house
where neighbors knew nothing.
Perished if they did.

Beneath one and a half concrete meters
another meter of earth
two and a half more of concrete
an extra shield

so his staff of one hundred
would be safe
from gas, bombs, tanks, everything
but the Boss.

II.

It's just as he would have left it—
labyrinth of doors
radio and maps for tracking battles
phone for barking orders
war room for combat chess

forbidden white sofa
on which he alone could rest.

For a few rubles I get to pose
in a Soviet uniform, salute
beneath Lenin's portrait

pick up that same phone
and pretend to be Stalin

try to avoid thinking about
the fates of nearly a thousand
who worked, visited here

or why it still took forty years
after one tyrant's death
to uncover
his hideaway

or how many other
buried secrets
might soon see daylight.

Slowly replacing that receiver
I listen
to the walls weep.

Baba Yaga

Russia's own witch
born as the three Zorya—
beautiful, benevolent goddesses

merging through centuries
into one evil cannibalistic one
the way the land she mothers

evolved from peasants, serfs, princes
to hammers, sickles, gulags
eventually Tsar Putin's proud nation.

Schoolchildren all know her
maybe mostly for that flying home
the famous hut on chicken legs

human jawbones for door latches
metatarsals for hinges, a forest setting
encircled by femur fencing, skull lanterns.

In all the stories the youngsters show up
sometimes on an impossible mission
sometimes as lost travelers not knowing

Baba Yaga favors blood cocktails
at Happy Hour. Hankers for maiden
mignon, appendix-on-rye, toe *borscht.*

Other times she falls for the lies
of kids who would shove her in the oven
and when they get what they want

the chicken legs race to a new spot
where she lifts off in her mortar
uses a pestle to grind at the sky.

Baba Yaga and Me

We both gnash teeth
all night. Sometimes all day

though unlike your iron set
this enamel is wearing away

cannot chomp through trees
when I long only to flee.

Whirling above birch tops
in our womb-like mortar

we screech at the wind
let it blow straggly hair

stiff as broomstick straw
needed to wipe away the trail

hide our origins in obscurity.
Mostly we treasure

those fowl legs—luxury
of moving the house

in any direction
southern morning exposure

shade rotating
to nourish the right herbs

later perfect sunset view
for watching my deer and rabbits

your three galloping horses.
Why drive when you can fly

descend in a different zone
maybe why I cackle

every time I land in Moscow
just the scent of Russia

making me giddy, ageless
as the Bony-Legged one.

We are so alike:
hungry for children

but craving just a taste
never the entire meal.

Nurturing when the mood strikes
fearsome when it doesn't

preferring to be mother to all
possessor of none.

In these last years I've acquired
my own magical hut

back turned to the forest
white fence made of tree bones

mortar and pestle in the garage
skulls flickering from posts

in a clear signal: do not enter
or I might consume you.

The neighbor kids know
there is no correct chant

to sway me. Would not dare
pass through this gate

that protects me here
in my own underworld.

Maiden's Island

They say Amazons
once lived here—
burnished bronze bodies brandishing spears

though their commands no longer echo
in these birch forests
at least no louder than ghosts

of the Khan's Golden Horde.
Wind whispers directions
guides me along a path

where sunlight plays tag
between quivering aspen leaves
and I half expect to see the women

but they have vanished
like all those tsars' sisters, wives, daughters
banished to convents in Siberia

except Catherine the Great
who wielded power with her pen
kept a firm grip on stately reins.

If only she'd hobbled her son
forced a bit into Paul's foaming mouth
put him out to pasture

before he could destroy the future
axing one gender
from the law of succession

and cannot help wonder now
who would control this island, this world
if her female descendants

had been permitted
to sail to other kingdoms
    spread
seeds, ideas, influence

become a bronze horde
spilling across earth
conquering   pillaging   raping
    winning.

Instead I hear only
wailing
of murdered *rusalki*
and then

    silence

before slipping silently, furtively
back to the Volga's shore
because it's not safe
for a woman

even a wild one

to wander alone
in a forest
she might have ruled.

Volga River

Woman of multiple moods
carved through forested hills
to engrave Russia

through centuries of invading
Khans, Tatars, Cossacks, Nazis

while maternally welcoming
seagulls, skiffs, barges, cruise ships

her silver birch spectators
lining the banks to clap
some prostrating themselves

while those of us gliding between
the emerald cleavage
grant imperial waves

to an audience
of fishermen, dachas, steamships

all of us floating as if between
an empress's benevolent bosom
interrupted only by sandbar nipples

and since Stalin decreed it
a series of cement monoliths
attempting to take temporary control
with triple-locked chastity belts.

Upstream a passionate Levitan
   once honored Mistress Russia
      by dressing Mother River

      with dabs of paint
          on a series of canvases
              intended to outlast us all

the way the water defies
all attempts to tame her

until open-mouthed at Volgograd

she is free at last

    legs spread wide
so sunsets
and sunrises
can alternate waltzes
              across the waves' dance floor

as she heads full tempo
for Astrakhan's simmering heat
then the cool delta of the Caspian
her presence overflowing
wide-hipped reservoirs
between breasted shores.

Reflections While Viewing Catherine the Great's Jewels

At Moscow's Diamond Fund
I am almost arrested
for being a poet
or at least the guard threatens

to take away my pen
use the notebook as evidence
perhaps believes I am here
to copy the crown's massive ruby

or more likely the scepter's
black Orlov diamond
in order to craft my own imitation
but I'd like to tell him

its owner—the Empress
who was gifted the giant gem
by her lover
was also addicted to writing

the most prolific case of hypergraphia
in the history of Russia's monarchy
and so when the suspicious man
reaches out to snatch the spiral pad

I do not give it up
do not do what she did in her early thirties
when accused of conspiring against Elizabeth
she was forced to toss her writings

into the flames. Sacrifice all
those thoughts, plans, reflections
to history's bowels. Instead
I do what she did *after* her coup

for nearly forty years
hoarding every last scrap
scribbling in every page's margin
producing stacks of manuscripts
keeping up voluminous correspondence

neither of us willing to surrender
a single word
to a tiny uniformed tyrant

instead preferring
to get revenge
by writing it all down
for posterity.

Living at The Five Corners, St. Petersburg, 2016

      I.

It is my temporary home
this urban wheel where five spokes converge
    and on this, my twentieth Russian visit
I stroll a different one each weekday

mix it up on weekends
the way it's prudent to avoid two museums in one day
    lest I get high on beauty

prefer these days to take my time
at everything.
      as if anyone notices

except maybe the pigeons
bobbing over to my whitewashed bench
to ascertain whether I've brought bread
from one of dozens of 24-hour stores.

A woman beside me polishes
her white shoes. A couple alternates
swigs from a bottle of designer water
and massive street cleaning machines
suddenly remind me of the *babushkas* of 1982

old women in floral scarves who swept
away the dirt with buckets of water
and twig brooms. It might be better
that they are no longer here to see this
that I'm still around to have become one of them.

II.

I am sipping a *latte* in my new favorite park
really a large handkerchief
stitched into a pocket-size square of trees
vanilla benches and trash cans in a perfect square
beneath fading spirea blooms
that remind me of the cascading bouquets
of all the brides I've seen this month
posed in front of St. Isaac's, Church on the Blood,
the Bronze Horseman, traditional sites
for conventional marriages

but today I idly watch
as people with leashed dogs board
modern green and white striped trolleys

until a man in a suit passes in front of me
carefully places his briefcase on the grass
begins to stroke a fledgling tree's bark
and then wraps his arms lovingly around the trunk

in a hug I wish I could give
to the entire Russian Federation

with or without the fallen away leaves
of its seaside republics.

III.

It could be ten in the evening
or three thirty in the morning
same pearlescent sky, veiled citrine sun

hope it's the former
since in the morning I plan to line up outside
the Hermitage's gold and black gate
make my way once more

to the giant tree girth
of the malachite columns
all that remains of Russia's
long since mined out mineral

except for the emerald-like shimmer
on the pigeons' necks
as they waddle in shade

and even when I exit in a slow shuffle
the birds barely move
in a gentle swirl
the way minnows wrap around legs, feet
yet never touch

so the green glitter dance
goes on in spite of me
as if they really do not notice.

Acknowledgments

Thanks to the following publications, in which some of these poems first appeared in this or an earlier version:

The Atlanta Review: "Happy Endings"
Colere: "Place of Wood"
Haight Ashbury Literary Journal: "A Russian Tale:1990"
Slipstream: "Soviet-Style Touring, 1982"
The 3288 Review: "The Russians Are Coming, 1962," "Touring the Ukraine, 1988," "Worshipping at Lenin's Mausoleum"
Whale Road Review: "Reflections While Viewing Catherine the Great's Jewels"

"The Amber Room" originally appeared in the collection *Looking for the Amber Room* (Emerald Unicorn Press).

Thanks to Ray, for all his help, suggestions, and faith in this book.

Cover photo, "Volga Church," by Judith A. Rypma; author photo by Ray Materson; cover and interior book design by Diane Kistner; PT Serif text and Macondo titling

About FutureCycle Press

FutureCycle Press is dedicated to publishing lasting English-language poetry books, chapbooks, and anthologies in both print-on-demand and Kindle ebook formats. Founded in 2007 by long-time independent editor/publishers and partners Diane Kistner and Robert S. King, the press incorporated as a nonprofit in 2012. A number of our editors are distinguished poets and writers in their own right, and we have been actively involved in the small press movement going back to the early seventies.

The FutureCycle Poetry Book Prize and honorarium is awarded annually for the best full-length volume of poetry we publish in a calendar year. Introduced in 2013, our Good Works projects are anthologies devoted to issues of universal significance, with all proceeds donated to a related worthy cause. Our Selected Poems series highlights contemporary poets with a substantial body of work to their credit; with this series we strive to resurrect work that has had limited distribution and is now out of print.

We are dedicated to giving all of the authors we publish the care their work deserves, making our catalog of titles the most diverse and distinguished it can be, and paying forward any earnings to fund more great books.

We've learned a few things about independent publishing over the years. We've also evolved a unique, resilient publishing model that allows us to focus mainly on vetting and preserving for posterity poetry collections of exceptional quality without becoming overwhelmed with bookkeeping and mailing, fundraising activities, or taxing editorial and production "bubbles." To find out more about what we are doing, come see us at www.futurecycle.org.